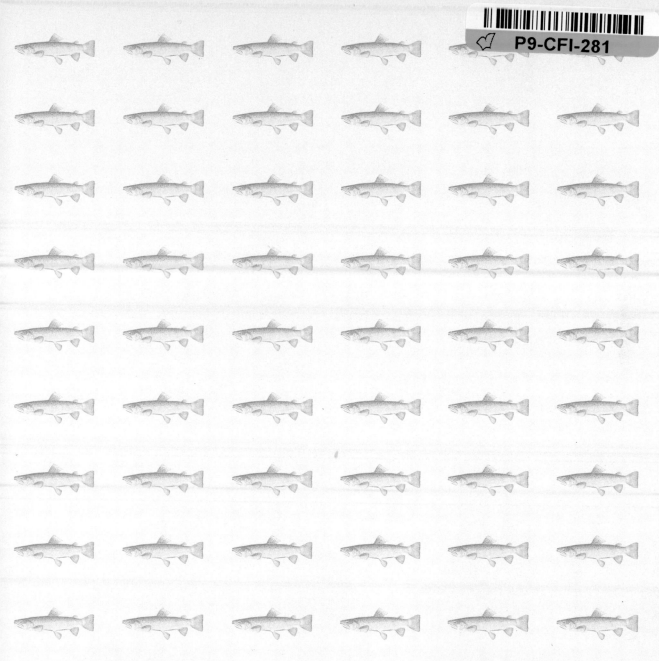

Fly Fishing

IN AMERICA

TAHOE TROUT [Salmo henshawi]

Fly Fishing

IN AMERICA

Tom Rosenbauer
in association with the American Museum of Fly Fishing
Introduction by Howell Raines

UNIVERSE PUBLISHING

APPLE PRESS

Acknowledgments

To Craig Gilborn and Ginny Hulett, executive director and executive assistant at the American Museum of Fly Fishing, for allowing us access to the museum's collection time and time again. Very special thanks to Jon Mathewson, curator of the collection, without whose special expertise and organization nothing would ever be found in the museum, and who has brought professionalism and organization to the museum's historic and valuable artifacts. To Randall Perkins, Kate Achor, and Margot Page, who produce *The American Fly Fisher*, the elegant magazine that brings the museum's collection to members around the world. Back issues of the magazine provided valuable detail, and Randall and Kate devoted much time to helping us track down the copyrights to some of the historical photographs.

      To Paul Wheeler of Apple Press for suggesting the idea. To designer Linda Carey for making everything look so terrific and editor Alexandra Mairs for constant attention to detail. To Paul Schullery for writing the only complete history of fly fishing in America, *American Fly Fishing: A History* (Lyons and Burford, 1987), a valuable resource for anyone intrigued by fly-fishing history.

Hardcover art, "Rocky Mountain Run" is from an original oil painting by Paco Young, available as a limited edition print from Applejack Limited Editions, Manchester, Vermont. Further information is available: (800) 969-1171.
Jacket front cover: East branch of the Delaware River in the Catskills
Jacket back cover: One of Preston Jennings's Iris streamers, which evolved from his studies of the spectrum and how it is perceived by trout and salmon

First published in the United States of America in 1996
by UNIVERSE PUBLISHING
A Division of Rizzoli International Publications, Inc.
300 Park Avenue South
New York, NY 10010

© 1996 Universe Publishing and Apple Press

96 97 98 99 / 10 9 8 7 6 5 4 3 2 1

Printed in Singapore

Library of Congress Catalog Card Number: 96-060688

CONTENTS

FOREWORD

Like other museums, the American Museum of Fly Fishing is a repository, a place where objects are kept and preserved. But it is more than that, although many people believe museums to be warehouses, as when the Smithsonian museums are said to be the "nation's attic." The museum also documents and interprets its holdings, and it assists researchers by providing access and information about its holdings.

Publication always deserves notice, but it's an event especially satisfying to the museum, since each book, catalogue and article is proof that the museum is more than a dusty attic, that, instead, it's both memory of and witness to fly fishing in its evolution as a sport with a long history and a literature perhaps second to none.

Craig Gilborn
Executive Director
The American Museum of Fly Fishing
Manchester, Vermont

INTRODUCTION

Nostalgia is a powerful, but tricky emotion. Especially in fishing, we are apt to look back at the early years of this century as a time of unrepeatable bounty. Yet there are trout living today in Catskill streams once choked to death by logging runoff. Like many New Yorkers, I cast for striped bass in the East River within sight of the Statue of Liberty. These examples attest to a fact that dawned on me as I was writing *Fly Fishing Through the Midlife Crisis*. We are living in the golden age of American fly fishing, in the sense that never before has the typical fly fisher had access to better equipment, better instruction, and more varied fishing locations.

I run into a few grumpy veterans who bemoan the democratization of the sport, but I side with Tom Rosenbauer in celebrating it. There are, of course, two stages to a fly-fishing education. The first has to do with learning how to fly fish. The second has to do with learning about the social history, geography, literature, and traditions described in *Fly Fishing in America*. Readers of this book will get an additional bonus in learning about the startling connection between fly fishing and Custer's Last Stand. But the more serious point is that if the nineteenth-century pioneers of American fly fishing could visit their old waters today, they would be surprised and, I suspect, pleased to discover that the United States is now home to both the most numerous and the most skilled fly fishers in the world.

My patriotic pride in that fact immediately summons a chastening thought planted by my fly-fishing mentor, Dick Blalock. He believed that competitiveness was alien to the spirit of fly fishing. I would add that it is tedious to exaggerate the importance of fly fishing. It is an elegant, but unessential pastime. Those of us who pursue it should not bore our friends and families about our good luck in living in a time when modern technology and travel have brought so much pleasure within reach.

But we can certainly celebrate our good luck and also remember the importance of a point made gently and unpreachily in these pages. A passion for fly fishing spurs us toward the indispensable work of preserving the environment. The spread of catch-and-release fishing, like the growing literature of fly fishing, has helped educate millions of us to become better custodians of this lovely, but battered planet and the waters that support our beguiling sport.

Howell Raines

THE ADIRONDACKS

GIANT BROOK
TROUT AND
TIRELESS
PROMOTERS

Fly fishing arrived in the North Woods just as the mayfly hatches do today: late but with a rush. By the middle of the nineteenth century the Adirondacks, with a vast number of placid lakes and ponds, were still very much a wilderness, yet one that railroads and luxury hotels in places like Lake George, just up the Hudson from Albany, made accessible and comfortable. Even though the rivers of Long Island and the Catskills were closer,

Pine Pond, the Adirondacks

ND NEW ENGLAND

the Adirondacks received far more press in the urban newspapers of the Northeast. Most notable of the Adirondack boosters was a New England minister named William H. H. Murray, known to his readers as "Adirondack Murray"; the thousands who, after reading his books, flocked to the Adirondacks from as far away as the Midwest were known as "Murray's Fools."

Typical of the prose that excited the sportsmen of the day comes from Murray's 1869 book *Adventures in the Wilderness: Or Camp-Life in the Adirondacks*:

Winslow Homer's creel, probably used on expedition at one of the Adirondack Great Camps

Being one of the first stops on the railoads north from Albany and New York City, Lake George was at one time host to dozens of luxury hotels. Although the town itself is busy with tourists, the lake is still a fly fisher's paradise.

Sebago Lake in Maine, still one of the finest places in the world for big brook trout and landlocked Atlantic salmon

But did you ever sit in a boat, with nine ounces of lance-wood for a rod, and two hundred feet of braided silk in your double-acting reel, and hook a trout whose strain brought tip and butt together as you checked him in some wild flight, and tested your quivering line from gut to reel-knot?

The period from about 1850 to 1880 was truly a golden age for Adirondack fly fishing. The native brook trout of this region, having evolved in less fertile waters than the European brown trout, were inclined to grab almost anything that looked remotely edible. Thus, the flies used in this region (and still popular in the Adirondacks today) were as gaudy as their names—the Royal Coachman, Red Ibis, Professor, Grizzly King, Parmacheene Belle. Winslow Homer fished with these patterns and about one-third of the watercolors he painted with Adirondack subjects were fly-fishing scenes. By the time he visited the Adirondacks, though, the tackle had become far more sophisticated. Fly reels were lighter, could carry more line, and had stronger drags, and the innovations that had come from technological developments in the Kentucky watch-making industry were also effected in New York and Vermont by such famous reel innovators as Billinghurst, Orvis, and Vom Hofe.

One of Winslow Homer's many fly reels, typically used by Victorian anglers

Equal in stature to the Adirondacks for the fly fisher of the nineteenth century were the big lakes and rivers of Maine, home to trophy brook trout and landlocked Atlantic salmon. The rush to Maine started about ten years after the Adirondack migration, but by the early 1890s Mary Orvis Marbury, daughter of the famous Vermont rodmaker Charles F. Orvis and head of the Orvis fly-tying operation, had no trouble obtaining detailed fly recommendations for Maine waters from sixteen anglers. She included these in her landmark book, *Favorite Flies and Their Histories*, which was the first book to standardize American fly patterns. (The book is still in print today, and the original flies that were reproduced in its colored plates are on display in the gallery of the American Museum of Fly Fishing.)

As fly fishers began to tangle with the bigger brook trout and landlocked salmon of Maine, a breakthrough in fly-rod design—the six-strip

Outlet of Pond-in-the-River, Maine

split-cane rod—let them land these fish in heavy water and cast farther than ever before. Split-cane rods are far stronger than the lancewood, greenheart, hickory, and ash rods that were preferred before the 1870s, when Samuel Phillipe of Easton, Pennsylvania, built the first split-cane rods. But it was Hiram Leonard of Maine who perfected the technique of producing rods on a commercial scale. Leonard brought Industrial Revolution principles to bamboo rod building and applied them to both rod and ferrule production. (He eventually moved his operation to downstate New York, so he could be closer to his wealthy clientele.)

A fly wallet, circa 1883, showing the colorful brook trout wet flies on gut snells, typical of the era. From three to as many as a dozen flies were attached to a single leader.

We think of the Maine woods as producing grizzled male guides, but history attaches far more importance to two women in the fly-fishing

Middle Dam, Rapid River, Maine, one of the many dams that creates a classic logging impoundment lake

lore of Maine. At the first annual Sportsmen's Show at Madison Square Garden in 1895, standing in the Maine exhibit was a six-foot woman in a Paris-designed hunting costume of lightweight green leather with a skirt that was a shocking seven inches above the floor. But Cornelia "Fly Rod" Crosby was no Victorian cheesecake—she had convinced the Maine Central Railroad to pay all of her expenses and to give her free rein to design the exhibit, which included a real Maine cabin full of stuffed deer and moose, giant mounted trout and salmon, and a huge collection of flies and tackle. Cornelia was the real thing—an accomplished shot who had been the guest of Buffalo Bill Cody in his private railroad car and had become friends with Annie Oakley. She

The brook trout was the main quarry of nineteenth-century Adirondack fly fishers. Today, rainbow trout introduced from California and brown trout from Europe are also pursued by fly fishers in this region.

later gave up her guiding career to become the first paid publicity agent for the state of Maine and did more to promote recreation in the Maine woods than anyone in history. In honor of her accomplishments, she was presented with guide license number one when Maine started to register guides.

Casting for stripers on a New England estuary. Most early New England saltwater fly fishing was done in estuaries like this one.

Scenes of Adirondack fishing lakes with typical brook trout wet flies of the 1890s. Note that the flies have snells attached to them so that three or more could be attached to the same leader.

*Cornelia "Fly Rod" Crosby, recipient of Maine's guide license number one,
shown here in a studio portrait in her Paris-designed fishing garb*

Because the large trout and salmon in Maine lakes feed primarily on the rainbow smelt, a long skinny baitfish, it is surprising that it took until the turn of the century for someone to develop artificial flies to seduce these fish. The singularly American development of these streamer flies occurred in the Rangeley Lakes area of Maine (these flies are still banned on many English rivers today because they are seen as being so crudely American—and deadly). In 1902 a Maine guide named Herb Welch developed the first fly that looked like our modern streamer, but the most famous—and most elegant—streamer patterns came from the hands of a woman named Carrie Stevens. Legend has it that one afternoon

A line winder from Winslow Homer's fishing tackle, used a hundred years ago for drying silk lines, which would rot if not dried after each use

An illustration from "Adirondack" Murray's 1869 Adventures in the Wilderness: Or Camp-Life in the Adirondacks, *which shows sportsmen from increasingly industrialized eastern cities venturing into the North Woods*

The brook trout is an environmentally sensitive fish from the char family and needs cold, clear spring water to survive. It has been pushed back into the most pristine waters, but even there it is threatened by acid precipitation.

FEMALE BROOK TROUT. (Salvelinus Fontinalis.)

in 1924 she had an inspiration and abandoned her housework to create the Gray Ghost, the most famous streamer of all time. Within an hour she had taken a six-pound, thirteen-ounce brook trout from the Upper Dam Pool at Mooselookmeguntic Lake. Demand for this streamer and the nearly twenty other patterns she created would soon exceed her ability to produce them.

Most of the giant brook trout of Maine and the Adirondacks are gone today, victims of acid rain, overfishing, and the introduction of exotic fish that compete for their sensitive niche in a relatively infertile habitat. But for the fly fisher willing to travel off the beaten path there are still big salmon and trout to be caught while being serenaded by the cries of a loon.

THE CATSKILLS

THE LITERARY TRADITION OF THE CATSKILLS

I t is not surprising that the Catskill Mountains of New York State have the richest literary tradition in American fly fishing. Just two hours by car from New York City today and perhaps a day's journey a hundred years ago, the Catskills hosted generations of fine writers who toiled in what is still the publishing capital of the world. The fly-fishing tradition in the Catskills has only developed in the twentieth century. In colonial days, the area was

The Willowemoc River, which together with the upper Beaverkill forms the big Beaverkill just below Roscoe, New York

The big Beaverkill in early spring at the Schoolhouse Pool. Most of the pools on the lower river have traditional names that date back fifty years or more.

Fishing a dry fly upstream on the Beaverkill, much as Theodore Gordon might have done at the turn of the century

distant and dangerous and there was plenty of good fly fishing on Long Island. (There is a story, probably apocryphal, about Daniel Webster having left church on a Sunday to capture a huge sea-run brook trout in the Carman's River on Long Island.) But soon railroads made it just as easy for nineteenth-century fly fishers to take a train to the Adirondacks, and this northern wilderness was popularized as the place for the sporting life, most likely because the Catskills were more heavily logged and would not appeal to sports like Winslow Homer who craved unspoiled hillsides with virgin white pines as much as they wanted a full creel.

Just before the turn of the century, European brown trout were introduced to the Catskills. The removal of large climax timber in the lower parts of the wider Catskill rivers had caused water temperatures to rise, which these new fish were better able to tolerate than the native brook trout. Many miles of new water thus became available to fly fishers. A selfish, consumptive hermit who weighed about ninety pounds in his wading brogues moved to the Catskills at the same time. Theodore Gordon was a prolific and talented correspondent who left behind many

Louis Rhead's reversed-tied flies are just one of his unique fly designs that seem not to have caught on with the fly fishers of his day.

THE BROWN TROUT. (Salmo Fario.)

The brown trout from Europe is more difficult to catch than the native brook trout. When it was introduced into the Catskills in the late nineteenth century it forced Catskill anglers to embrace a more technical system of fly tying that sought to imitate aquatic insects more precisely.

The Beaverkill, although heavily fished and entwined with a superhighway, still offers prolific fly hatches and challenging fishing.

letters and magazine articles about his adaptation of the more imitative English fly patterns to our faster, infertile mountain rivers. Gordon's writing was rediscovered by a group of New York City anglers in the 1940s, and John McDonald, an editor with *Fortune* magazine, compiled a complete volume of Gordon's articles and letters called *The Complete Fly Fisher*. Although Gordon's dry flies were refined by such Catskill fly tiers as the two husband-and-wife teams, Walt and Winnie Dette and Harry and Elsie Darbee, between the 1930s and the 1980s, what we call "traditional dry flies" today still owe a great deal to Gordon's experimentation and correspondence with fly tiers both in the United States and in England.

Theodore Gordon on his beloved Neversink River, with an unidentified mystery woman (the only woman besides his mother ever mentioned in his writing). Framed below are authentic Gordon flies from the Cushner collection of the American Museum of Fly Fishing.

It is ironic that another fly-fishing writer of the same period, Louis Rhead, who was not only a prolific writer, an extremely innovative fly tier, and a successful commercial illustrator, but also a skilled self-promoter, is almost unknown today. He wrote four fishing books and edited two others, but it is perhaps because of his most ambitious book, *American Trout Stream Insects*, that he is ignored today. The book offered

Late spring on the Beaverkill

superb illustrations of all the life stages of our major trout stream insects, but unfortunately Rhead, an arrogant researcher, refused to identify insects by their scientific names and made up his own, thus rendering the book unusable to anglers from other regions and in future years.

It wasn't until 1935 that Preston Jennings's *A Book of Trout Flies*, the first modern guide to trout stream insects and their imitations, was published by the Derrydale Press. Jennings had secured the assistance of the most prominent entomologists of the era, and thus was truly the father of the scientific imitationist theory of fly fishing and fly tying that we still follow today. In contrast to Jennings was another New Yorker and Catskill fly fisher, George LaBranche, who believed that the position of a fly on the water and its movement and size were far more important than its

color or pattern. LaBranche's theories on dry-fly fishing were codified in his 1914 book *The Dry Fly and Fast Water*, which further reinforced Gordon's idea that the fast mountain streams of the United States require different techniques and fly patterns than the gentle meadow streams of England. Both books are delightful reading and still contain valuable advice for the modern fly fisher.

The Catskills witnessed a golden age of fly fishing from 1930 to 1960, due to a couple of factors. One was that there were a number of wealthy New Yorkers living and fishing in the Catskills, who had both time to experiment with fishing techniques and the resources to get their writing published.

Edward Hewitt typified the wealthy Catskill fly fisher of the first half of the twentieth century: a lifelong tinkerer of tackle, technique, and flies, who wrote well and often of his experiments.

George LaBranche was a contemporary of Hewitt, but unlike Hewitt, he was much more concerned with technique and the behavior of a fly on the water than with precise imitation.

Among the most notable was Edward Ringwood Hewitt. A tireless experimenter whose father was once mayor of New York City, Hewitt spent most of his time in a cabin on the Neversink River. He was a strong proponent of big, bushy, attractor dry flies called spiders, and he also did much to popularize the technique of artificial nymph fishing, using a form of wet fly that is much more suggestive of specific immature forms of aquatic insects on which trout do most of their feeding.

Another reason the Catskills produced so much of our fly-fishing tradition is that many enthusiastic fly fishers were New York publishers who befriended local fly fishers. One of the most notable was Art Flick, a tavern owner from Westkill, New York, who was encouraged by the New York publishing community to write *Art Flick's Streamside Guide* in 1947, a tiny vest-pocket guide to Catskill mayfly hatches that is still one of the best-selling fly-fishing books of all time.

By far the two writers most influential in cementing the Catskill tradition were Arnold Gingrich, the urbane founding publisher of *Esquire* magazine, and Alfred Waterbury Miller, better known by his pen name, Sparse Grey Hackle. Indeed, Gingrich was quoting Sparse when he penned one of his most famous lines:

As Sparse Grey Hackle says, some of the best fishing is to be found not in water but in print. It follows that some of the best fishing partners are to be found not in life but in literature. I know there are some things I've read that come to mind more often while I'm fishing than anything I can remember that anybody ever said to me beside stream or pond.

Fishing on the Beaverkill at the turn of the century

Gingrich, primarily through his books *The Well-Tempered Angler*, *The Fishing in Print*, and *The Joys of Trout*, gave us our modern literary and ethical fly-fishing conscience, most of it slanted toward eastern, in particular Catskill, traditions. Sparse was the editor of the Angler's Club of New York Bulletin for decades and his 1971 book *Fishless Days, Angling Nights* chronicles

Lee Wulff, known as the father of catch-and-release fishing, lived out his last years on the upper Beaverkill.

fifty years of Catskill fly fishing, including memories of fishing with Hewitt and LaBranche. The main reason Miller used a pen name is that he was an early environmental crusader but needed to protect his livelihood as a Wall Street reporter and consultant. His greatest cause was protecting the Beaverkill against the construction of Route 17, and it is likely that he had a hand in this quote from the April 1, 1964, *New York Herald Tribune*: "A six-lane highway running through the Valley of the Beaverkill, crossing the stream with 11 bridges in 26 miles, and in the opinion of many, ruining the historic river as a trout fisherman's shrine."

Route 17 did not ruin the fishing in the Beaverkill, but it probably contributed to the lowering of its water table and the degradation of its trout-spawning tributaries. And, the most popular pool on the Beaverkill, Cairns's Pool, is crossed at its head by a massive bridge. Still, the Beaverkill and surrounding Catskill rivers do offer some of the finest trout fishing in the East, especially to the angler who appreciates fishing beside the ghosts of some of the most important figures in American fly-fishing history.

THE MIDWEST

THE SPRING-FED RIVERS OF PENNSYLVANIA AND THE MIDWEST

I t comes as no surprise that many of the earliest references to fly fishing in the United States are from Pennsylvania. Until after the Civil War, fishing for sport was regarded as a pursuit of the idle, rich or otherwise, and was often considered of the same ilk as horse racing. Pennsylvania, with its long history of religious and social tolerance, was probably one place where fly fishing could be pursued with a minimum of

Fishing Creek, Pennsylvania

guilt. By the time the Declaration of Independence was signed, Philadelphia had at least three fishing clubs with hundreds of members, and also had three fishing-tackle outlets, the most famous of which was owned by Edward Pole and offered "artificial flies, moths, and hackles, with suitable lines of any length."

Although there is no doubt fly fishing was practiced in the mountain streams of Potter County and in the Poconos, where the famous Henryville Club on the Brodhead still exists, most of the writing about

The delicacy of a mayfly on the water demonstrates why Pennsylvania and Michigan fly fishers searched for a better imitation than standard bushy hackled dry flies.

Letort Spring Run, which runs through Carlisle, Pennsylvania, has figured prominently in the history of American fly fishing for almost two hundred years. Its waters are not as cold and clear as they were a hundred years ago, but the river still holds large and difficult brown trout.

Pennsylvania trout fishing focused on the limestone streams of south-central Pennsylvania. One of the first American fly-fishing correspondents for sporting periodicals, George Gibson, fished the Letort and other spring-fed streams around the Harrisburg area. Unfortunately, little survives of his writing or of the early historical records of Pennsylvania fly fishing.

It was not until the 1950s that a true revolution in fly-fishing technique came out of Pennsylvania. Vincent Marinaro's first book, *A Modern Dry-Fly Code*, is considered one of the most influential books in twentieth-century fly fishing. Marinaro developed a new style of tying the dry fly that placed the wings of a mayfly imitation further back along the body and split the tails widely. Anglers had known that mayflies looked more like this for centuries but most fly tiers had been blindly following the designs of their predecessors. Perhaps even more important were Marinaro's precise imitations of land-borne insects or "terrestrials." Fly fishers had known for hundreds of years that trout eat ants, beetles, and grasshoppers, but none had gone to the lengths Marinaro had, both in observing the feeding behavior of the trout to these insects and their mutations. Marinaro was also a pioneer in fishing tiny flies and included his "jassid," or leafhopper imitation, in a broad classification of "minutiae," or tiny flies pinioned in the surface film.

Marinaro's circle of friends included other fly-fishing innovators who would become almost as well known. Charlie Fox, Marinaro's friend

Joe Brooks's fishing vest. Brooks did much to popularize the No-Hackle flies, which were developed by Michigan anglers Doug Swisher and Carl Richards.

The Letort now runs through suburban backyards, but in many places one can catch wild trout in lush surroundings as anglers have for over two hundred years.

The Adams dry fly, the most popular fly in use today, was developed on Michigan trout streams.

and neighbor, wrote *This Wonderful World of Trout* (1963) and *Rising Trout* (1967), which were less innovative than Marinaro's books but became just as popular. There was also a young college student named Ernest Schwiebert who fished with this gang of Letort regulars and wrote *Matching the Hatch* in 1955, the first transcontinental guide to North American mayfly hatches.

The Midwest, although lacking the mountains that we commonly associate with trout streams, is blessed with glacial deposits that hold cold groundwater like a sponge. Thus, Ohio, Michigan, Wisconsin, and Minnesota have fly-fishing legacies that most often involve trout. From Minnesota comes the Muddler Minnow, which is usually associated with the Rocky Mountains. The fly was adapted by Don Gapen in the 1930s from a simpler pattern used by local Indians to capture the huge brook trout of the Nipigon River in Ontario. Minnesota also produced George Leonard Herter and his huge and amusing *Herter's Catalog*, which was probably the inspiration

The Hornberg fly, best known today in New England, was actually developed by a Wisconsin game warden.

The Pere Marquette River is typical of the rivers of Michigan: smooth and clear, yet with a surprisingly fast current.

Fishing for smallmouth bass on the Susquehanna River

for generations of would-be fly tiers. Historically, though, his catalog muddied the record, as Herter was a master of hyperbole and claimed to be the originator of about half of the inventions known to fly fishers at the time.

Serious backwoods brook trout fishers in Maine and New Hampshire will be surprised to learn that their favorite New England fly, the Hornberg, was originated by a Wisconsin game warden. It's amazing to many people today that during the 1930s and early 1940s Stevens Point, Wisconsin, was the commercial fly-tying capital of the world, with a host of companies producing over ten million flies a year, all tied by hand.

When spin fishing became widely available after World War II, making fish easier to catch, the fly industry collapsed and most of the Stevens Point fly factories closed their doors.

Michigan originated both the most popular dry fly of all time and the modern

Early fly fishing in Lanesboro, Minnesota

revolution in dry-fly design. In 1922 Leonard Halliday tied a fly for an Ohio attorney named Charles Adams to use on the Boardman River. Adams liked the fly, Halliday named it for him, and since then millions have been tied. It is still the most popular dry-fly pattern in North America. Fifty years later, Joe Brooks, one of America's most beloved fly-fishing writers, met Carl Richards and Doug Swisher, young anglers who had been studying and photographing mayfly hatches throughout the country, but especially in their home state of Michigan. Brooks wrote an article in *Outdoor Life* in 1970 about their tiny imitations of mayflies that dispensed with expensive and hard-to-obtain chicken hackle. A year later their book was published, beginning a revolution with the first clear, close-up color photographs of mayflies and many new innovative fly patterns. In the twenty-five years since its publication, fly tying and fly fishing have changed and grown dramatically, with far more emphasis on imitating specific insects and other game fish foods than ever before.

The Michigan grayling, a relict type of arctic grayling that once existed in northern Michigan, is now extinct due to extensive logging and overfishing. But it is still possible to catch wild brown and brook trout on the Ausable and wild steelhead on the Pere Marquette if one doesn't mind dodging the canoes. And although the Letort has suffered from chemical spills from commercial watercress farms in its upper reaches, it remains one of the most fascinating spring creeks in the world.

Vincent Marinaro casting to a rising trout on a Pennsylvania spring creek

THE WEST

TROUT FISHING
IN THE ROCKIES

Some historians feel that fly fishing was partly to blame for the demise of Lieutenant Colonel George Armstrong Custer. It seems that Brigadier General George Crook was heading north against the Sioux at the same time Custer was chasing them to the south. But Crook, recently forced to withdraw after a humiliating encounter with the Sioux, decided to camp along Goose Creek in Wyoming's Bighorn Mountains instead of continuing his pursuit. Crook, a serious sportsman, just hap-

*The Henry's Fork of the
Snake River at Last Chance, Idaho*

pened to have several fine split-bamboo fly rods with him, and the cut-throat trout fishing was so good that he and his men caught sixty to eighty trout per day. Eight days later, when Custer and five companies of the Seventh Cavalry were massacred, Crook was still fishing.

Unfortunately, we don't know which fly patterns were most successful for Crook.

The very first settlers in the American West had little time for fly fishing, but it wasn't long before scientists, soldiers, and other travelers who had both time and the luxury of carrying a little extra gear like fly-fishing tackle began to sample the untouched trout fishing of the

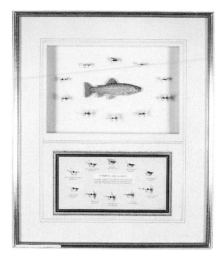

Flies tied by Dan Bailey, a twentieth-century pioneer of Montana trout fishing. The Rocky Mountain style personified by Bailey's flies uses hackle and hair for wings and tails, instead of feathers.

Rockies. This was before rainbows were carried over the mountains from the Pacific Coast and before brown trout were brought from Scotland and Germany via hatcheries in New York State and Michigan, so all of the earliest trout fishing was for the various subspecies of cutthroats. It was the railroads, however, that brought great numbers of sportsmen to the Rockies. By the 1890s wealthy fly fishers bought land along such famous rivers as the Henry's Fork at Last Chance, Idaho.

By the 1930s, rainbow and brown trout had been established in

Today, fly fishing is a year-round pastime in the Rocky Mountains.

most of the river systems of the Rockies, and local fly patterns emerged, like the famous Bunyan Bug and the Potts Mite series, made of woven hair from skunk, badger, and deer by Franz Pott, a barber and wig maker from Missoula, Montana. But it was emigrants from both coasts who started to codify the fishing traditions of the Rockies. In 1933, a Californian named Don Martinez opened a small fly shop in West Yellowstone, Montana. He was a keen observer of aquatic insects and developed many flies specifically for western waters, the most famous of which was the Woolly Worm, one of the most popular flies in trout streams throughout the world.

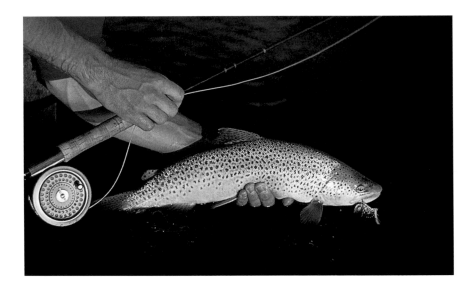

The Madison River in Montana (above) offers some of the finest trout fishing in the world, despite very high fishing pressure. Although most of the river is under catch-and-release regulations, its rainbow trout population has been ravaged in recent years by whirling disease, a bacterial parasite. Brown trout (facing page, below) are far more resistant to the disease, and it is hoped that the Madison's rainbows will develop an equally effective natural immunity.

But it was another 1930s emigrant, Dan Bailey, who became the most widely known Rocky Mountain fly fisher of the twentieth century. Bailey, a physics professor from New York City, owned a fly shop on Main Street, which, with its "Wall of Fame" tracings of monstrous trout, became a touchstone for any fly fisher traveling to Montana. (His son still carries on the business today, and John Bailey is known as one of the most savvy businessmen and ardent conservationists in the business.) Dan Bailey typified the Montana fly fisher of the middle of the twentieth century as contrasted to the eastern establishment fly fishers. One of Bailey's longtime

The Henry's Fork of the Snake River in Idaho has been the testing ground of many innovative fly patterns, especially those designed for difficult, selectively feeding trout. Its rich, weedy streambed has been called an insect factory.

The rugged Yellowstone River in Montana, home river of Dan Bailey and the inspiration for many of the bigger "meat" flies designed to provoke trout rather than imitate a specific insect

friends was an eastern fly fisher named Preston Jennings, who wrote the first modern book of insect imitations, *A Book of Trout Flies*. When Jennings wrote to Bailey in 1954 and asked him about his theories of imitation, Bailey responded:

> As long as a dry fly floats well and comes fairly close to imitating a large group of insects it does the trick. Changes which I have made in flies have been based on the trout's acceptance. That being the case, my patterns might look less like the natural than English or Eastern flies.

TAHOE TROUT (SALMO HENSHAWI)

The cutthroat trout is the only true native trout of the Rocky Mountains. It was first scientifically recognized by Lewis and Clark.

In the 1970s the focus of new developments in fly fishing shifted from the streams of the Catskills and the Pennsylvania limestone streams to the trout-rich tailwaters of the Rockies, rivers that were originally great trout streams made even better and more challenging by the manic development of water projects in the first half of the twentieth century.

In the Rockies, fishing opportunities became more readily avail-

The Firehole River flows entirely within Yellowstone National Park and although it carries the runoff of Old Faithful and other thermal wonders, the river stays cold enough to support trout because its headwaters are on a high plateau that might have snow twelve months a year.

able to the average tourist through air travel and a greatly expanded network of professional guides. With the guides and the tourist fly fishers came increased business opportunities, and thus both local fly fishers and transplanted easterners were able to make a living in the fly-fishing business. These personalities were able to experiment with fly patterns and techniques in a very diverse and productive fishery, as the West has more fly-fishing opportunities over a season than any place else in the world. With enlightened management and a strong grass-roots support for trout habitat, trout fishing in the Rockies, while not what it was in Dan Bailey's time, is amazingly productive in relation to the pressure it receives by a large population of fly fishers.

Fishing in the early 1890s on Williams Fork at Middle Park, Colorado

Although fly fishing came late to the Rockies, this Victorian-era photo of the Roaring Fork in Colorado shows that once the trains came, so did fishing for sport instead of subsistence.

A photograph from the Mary Orvis Marbury 1892 fly plates entitled
"Montana Trout." It is safe to assume that most Montana trout fishing trips a
century ago were not as elegantly equipped.

*Early fly fishers in Yellowstone National Park were amazed to be able to catch
cutthroat trout in the ice cold waters of Yellowstone Lake and then promptly poach them
on the spot in a boiling fumarole at their feet. This photo dates from the 1890s.*

THE NORTHWEST

THE CHALLENGE OF STEELHEAD FISHING

Prior to 1850, adventurers traveling to the Far West expressed frustration at their lack of success with fly-fishing tackle. Captain George B. McClellan, as a member of a railroad survey in 1853, complained in his diary about the fish in a Yakima Valley lake in what is now Washington State: "the wretches would not rise to a fly." As

Not all West Coast fly fishing uses shooting heads and long casts. Here, a lone angler fishes a meadow stream that feeds into a mountain lake.

the railroads came closer to linking both coasts, fly fishers from the East and from England began to write of more consistent success with the fly rod. Charles Hallock, founding editor of *Forest & Stream* magazine, wrote glowingly of the fishing in the Lake Tahoe and Yosemite areas in his 1873 book *The Fishing Tourist*. He urged the fishing tourist to "find his way to virgin lakes and streams where artificial has never trailed, and whose silvery trout have no suspicion of wiles or stratagems."

Despite wonderful and varied trout fishing on the West Coast, it has been the anadromous fish species, the steelhead or ocean-run race of rainbow trout, and to a lesser degree the five species of Pacific salmon,

THE RAINBOW TROUT. (Salmo Irideus.)

The steelhead, a race of rainbow trout that lives in the ocean and returns to freshwater rivers to spawn, figures prominently in the history of West Coast fly fishing.

Rivers like the Deschutes in Oregon demonstrate why West Coast fly fishers are obsessed with distance casting.

that have contributed most to the fly-fishing traditions of the Pacific Coast. A young Rudyard Kipling, on his first trip to America in 1889, talked of capturing a twelve-pound steelhead from the Clackamas River in Oregon with the same reverence modern steelhead anglers have for their quarry (but without their catch-and-release ethics):

I stepped into the shallows and heaved him out with a respectful hand under the gill, for which kindness he battered me about the legs with his tail, and I felt the strength of him and was proud. I was dripping with sweat, spangled like a harlequin with scales, wet from the waist down, nose peeled by the sun, but utterly, supremely, and consumately happy.

Because steelhead are often caught in the lower reaches of powerful mountain rivers, casting great distances has always been an obsession with California fly fishers in particular, and to this day some of the most elegant and powerful casters in the country are members of the Golden Gate Casting Club, which was formed in 1893. Along with improved casting techniques and bigger rods came the uniquely far-western innovation called the shooting head, a fly line that sacrifices delicacy for brute power. With this new line, fly fishers could double both the distance and the depth of their presentations. Fly-casting distance records up until 1894 were all won by New Yorkers, but in that year an eighty-one-foot cast by a Californian won a national casting tournament. For the next twenty years the record went back and forth from California to Chicago to New York. In the second half of this century, distance-casting records have been dominated by Californians.

The steelhead fly has undergone a remarkable process of evolution in the past one hundred years. Both Victorian-era featherwing salmon flies and oversized versions of eastern brook trout wet flies were

used with some success. Most knowledgable fly fishers, however, used modifications of these flies, replacing feather wings by bucktail and polar bear hair, which is bulkier, more durable, and better able to survive the boiling currents of intimidating rivers like the Eel, Umpqua, and Rogue. Zane Grey urged Joe Wharton, his local mentor and tackle provider, to stock English and Scottish fly tackle in his hardware store in Grant's Pass, Oregon, even though Grey preferred Wharton's own simpler flies.

For the most part, the steelhead fly-fishing tradition developed from a blue-collar perspective that was far different from the privileged background of most eastern and English fly fishers. Also, because bait and hardware have always been allowed on steelhead rivers (unlike most Atlantic salmon rivers which are reserved for fly fishing only), steelhead fly fishers have been looser and more innovative. By the 1940s steelhead flies had evolved to the point where they had a style and look of their own, and patterns such as Jim Pray's Optic series, Ken McLeod's Skykomish Sunrise and Purple Bell, and Enos Bradner's Brad's Brat had

The North Umpqua was a favorite steelhead river of Zane Grey.

A big lake rainbow peels line off a reel in a strong run.

become standards that are still among the most popular steelhead flies in use today. The flies are brash, colorful, and durable, a reflection of both the pragmatic values of the men who created them and the untamed waters in which they were fished.

These homegrown flies all had the same proportions and profile and were fished as deep as possible on sinking lines. But twenty years ago, a revolution in steelhead fly tying took place. Dry flies became popular and a small group of fly fishers began to realize the effectiveness of oversize trout nymphs. The most exciting and artistic part of this renaissance came from the fly-tying vise of Syd Glasso of Forks, Washington. Glasso borrowed the Spey style of Atlantic salmon fly directly from England and invented his own versions with colors and sizes more suitable to steelhead. The resulting patterns are among the most elegant flies ever created for any type of fishing, and Glasso's many admirers continue the innovations he started. Even the most chauvinistic English fly dresser would have to admit that the most beautiful Spey flies today come from the Pacific Northwest.

Steelhead fishing today in the Northwest is a shadow of its former glory. Netting, overfishing, dams, and perhaps unknown factors out

Letcher Lambuth's line winder, used to wind fly rod guides in 1920s Seattle

The Clackamas at the turn of the century. It is still a famous river today,
but netting and dams have taken a toll on its steelhead fishery.

in the open ocean where steelhead spend most of their lives have caused an alarming decline in population. Still, for the persistent fly fisher, steelhead are one of the most exciting fish that will rise to the fly, and the rivers they ascend for their spawning runs are satisfying to the souls of our increasingly urban population.

SALTWATER FLY F

SALTWATER FLY FISHING NORTH AND SOUTH

A sign of the lack of historical perspective by today's fly fishers is the platitude "the new frontier of saltwater fly fishing." It is true that technological improvements such as the fiberglass fly rod in the 1950s and, even more important, the graphite fly rod in the 1970s made forty-pound striped bass and even 185-pound tarpon a realistic goal on a tiny fly. The bamboo

Modern flats fishing in Florida is a far cry from early explorations with a fly rod.

SHING

rods used prior to 1950 could not hold large saltwater species without breaking, but smaller saltwater gamefish have been taken with a fly in the United States for well over 150 years.

Although they did not fish in the crashing surf as today's fly-rod striped bass enthusiasts do, probably because of the limitations of nineteenth-century tackle in brisk winds, fly rodders were catching striped bass in New England estuaries at least as early as 1849. Frank Forester said of striped bass in his *Frank Forester's Fish and Fishing*: "but any of the well-known salmon flies will secure him, as will the scarlet-bodied fly with scarlet ibis and silver pheasant wings." And Robert Barnwell Roosevelt, black-sheep uncle of Theodore, was unequivocal in his 1862 book *Game Fish of the North* when he stated that "the most scientific and truly sportsmanlike mode of taking striped bass must be admitted to be with the fly."

Striped bass fishing with a fly seems to have gone through pulses of activity and rediscovery, which is quite understandable since the fish themselves go through cyclic periods of abundance. It was not until the 1940s that modern pioneers like Hal Lyman and Frank Woolner, both founding editors of *Saltwater Sportsman* magazine, and Harold and Frank Gibbs, known for the Gibbs Striper fly, began to popularize striped bass fishing with a fly. Still, it remained a pastime restricted mostly to local anglers in Massachusetts and Rhode Island until the late 1980s. At that time, a fifty-pound striped bass on a fly became a reality, due to rebounding stocks of stripers, new flies designed to imitate striped bass food more

A trophy Joe Brooks received in a Florida tarpon tournament

It was not until fly rods and reels were made from strong space-age materials that a tarpon this size could be landed with fly tackle.

Bowing the rod to a large tarpon in the Florida Keys

specifically, and graphite rods, improved fly lines, and leader materials.

Modern challenges in saltwater fly fishing include the pursuit of bonefish as the sole quarry on a fishing trip, the attempt to catch a tarpon over 150 pounds on a fly, and the capture of a permit on a fly. But the capture of these subtropical species on a fly, mainly in Florida, was not unheard of a hundred years ago. James Henshall, in his 1884 book *Camping and Cruising in Florida*, wrote of catching many species of saltwater fish on a fly, including tarpon, jacks, seatrout, redfish, bluefish, snook, and ladyfish, as well as freshwater largemouth bass. Less than ten years later, a correspondent named Maxie wrote to *Forest & Stream* magazine about the fine sport he had fly fishing for bonefish in Biscayne Bay near Miami using "a medium-weight fly rod with large, gaudy salmon or bass flies."

A Gibbs Striper fly, a popular pattern for striped bass in the mid-twentieth century

At the turn of the century, a father-and-son team named A. W. and Julian Dimock published *Book of the Tarpon*, featuring incredible black-and-white photographs of leaping tarpon that are the envy even of today's outdoor photographers. They were wise in their tackle selection advice: "Proportion your tackle to the work to be done. A fly rod with stiff action fits a baby tarpon down to the ground, but even a five-pounder will tow you for a mile through a creek before you can tire him with the spring of the rod." With today's graphite rods, disc drag reels, and superb leader materials, a five-pound tarpon can be brought to hand in a couple of minutes without having to follow it with the boat, but the Dimocks' philosophy of how to handle the fish would be appreciated by Florida guides of the 1990s. They urged the reader: "Don't carry a gaff. Don't murder your game. To object to taking a tarpon for mounting or other rational purpose would be fanatical, but wantonly to slay the beautiful, harmless creatures

that have contributed to your pleasure is not only cruel, but it is unfair to your fellow sportsmen."

The Long Key Fishing Club was organized in 1917 in the Florida Keys, and members included Zane Grey, Herbert Hoover, and Andrew Mellon. Although they mostly used revolving-spool Vom Hofe reels instead of more conventional fly reels (fly reels then did not have the stopping power of modern reels, and besides, Edward Vom Hofe was a member of the club), they used 9 1/2- to 10-foot bamboo fly rods and caught tarpon, bonefish, permit, sailfish, wahoo, kingfish, amberjack, and barracuda—although many of the flies may have been trolled rather than cast to feeding fish.

Just before World War II, a guide named Bill Smith was criticized

Despite modern tackle, most anglers on the Florida flats require professional guides who can spot bonefish hundreds of yards away.

by George LaBranche for catching bonefish on a pork rind lure and calling it fly fishing (LaBranche himself had never taken a bonefish on a fly). Smith promptly proceeded to catch a bonefish on a simple white fly and had his picture taken for the local newspapers with his catch. Bill's wife, Bonnie, was also a guide who convinced her two sisters, Beulah and Frankee, to move to Florida and taught them how to guide. After the war, an outdoor writer named Joe Brooks, who did more to popularize saltwater fly fishing than anyone else in the twentieth century, claimed to have

caught the first bonefish intentionally on a fly outfit, but he knew the Smiths and it is not known why Bill did not contest this claim. Still, Brooks caught what is most likely the first permit taken intentionally on fly tackle while guided by Bonnie Smith. And in 1947 LaBranche, by then an old man, was guided into his first bonefish on a fly by Frankee Albright, Bonnie's sister.

In the past two decades, instead of a couple of personalities and a half-dozen guides who specialize in fly fishing as it was in the 1940s, there are scores of talented personalities and hundreds of guides who specialize in saltwater fly fishing. Modern innovations have made it possible for even a relatively unskilled fly fisher to catch a bonefish, permit, or even a tarpon over one hundred pounds on fly tackle. Although the pressure on the resources of all fisheries has increased greatly in the past half-century, more and more states are recognizing the economic value of many ocean species, particularly the inshore varieties, and are giving gamefish status to fish like the striped bass,

Beulah Cass, Bonnie Smith, and Frankie Albright

redfish, and snook. The setting of minimum sizes for redfish and striped bass in the early 1990s and the gill net ban in Florida in the mid-1990s are testaments to the efforts of concerned organized sportsmen's groups.

PHOTOGRAPHY CREDITS

Cover: Richard Franklin
Back cover: Gary Clayton Hall
page 2   Gary Clayton Hall
6   The American Museum of Fly Fishing
9   Richard Franklin

The Adirondacks and the Northeast:
10-11   Jim Lepage
12   The American Museum of Fly Fishing (top)
12   Tom Rosenbauer (bottom)
13   Jim Lepage
14   The American Museum of Fly Fishing
14-15   Jim Lepage
16   The American Museum of Fly Fishing
17   Jim Lepage
18-19   Barry and Cathy Beck
19   The American Museum of Fly Fishing
20   The American Museum of Fly Fishing
21   The American Museum of Fly Fishing
22   The American Museum of Fly Fishing (top and bottom)
23   Gary Clayton Hall

The Catskills:
24-25   Dale C. Spartus/The Green Agency
26   Dale C. Spartus/The Green Agency
27   Richard Franklin
28   Gary Clayton Hall (top and bottom)
29   Richard Franklin
30   Gary Clayton Hall
31   Richard Franklin
32   The American Museum of Fly Fishing
33   The American Museum of Fly Fishing
34   The American Museum of Fly Fishing
35   The American Museum of Fly Fishing

The Midwest:
36-37   Barry and Cathy Beck
38   Barry and Cathy Beck
39   Nathan Bilow
40   Gary Clayton Hall
41   Barry and Cathy Beck (top)
41   The American Museum of Fly Fishing (bottom)

42   The American Museum of Fly Fishing (top)
42   Tom Rosenbauer (bottom)
43   Barry and Cathy Beck
44   The American Museum of Fly Fishing
45   The American Museum of Fly Fishing

The West:
46-47   Richard Franklin
48   Gary Clayton Hall
49   Nathan Bilow
50   Derek Mitchell (bottom)
51   Richard Franklin
52   Dale C. Spartus/The Green Agency
53   Barry and Cathy Beck
54   Gary Clayton Hall
55   Victor H. Colvard/The Green Agency
56   The American Museum of Fly Fishing
57   Gary Clayton Hall
58   The American Museum of Fly Fishing
59   The American Museum of Fly Fishing

The Northwest:
60-61   Brian O'Keefe
62   Gary Clayton Hall
63   Jim Lepage
65   Brian O'Keefe
66   Brian O'Keefe
67   Brian O'Keefe
68   Gary Clayton Hall
69   The American Museum of Fly Fishing

Saltwater Fly Fishing:
70-71   Barry and Cathy Beck
72   Gary Clayton Hall
73   Dale C. Spartus/The Green Agency
74   Dale C. Spartus/The Green Agency
75   Gary Clayton Hall
76   Barry and Cathy Beck
77   Barry and Cathy Beck
78   Dale C. Spartus/The Green Agency
79   Ben Estes